HOW TO GET OVER HIM

How To Get Over Him

A MANUAL FOR WOMEN TO HELP YOU MOVE PAST THE WRONG GUY

by Multi-Award Winning Author,
Dr. Christine Topjian

Authors Get Published Publishing

Contents

Copyright Information ... vii
A Note From the Author ... ix

Pre-Intro and Some Understandings — 1

Introduction ... 6
1 The Good Wrong Guy ... 14
2 Chin Up ... 21
3 Activating Through Prayer ... 30
4 Feelings Are Fickle and Fleeting ... 38
5 If the Answer Is No, Know That There Is a "Yes" Coming! ... 55
6 Prepare Yourself ... 64
7 Staying Gorgeous ... 72
8 Getting Over Him....Little By Little ... 77
9 Closeness To God ... 86
10 Success! ... 93

Pay It Forward ... 95

About Dr. Topjian 99
Other Books From the Author 101

Copyright Information

Published by Christine Topjian Publishing
(An Imprint of Authors Get Published)

www.DrChristineTopjian.com

www.AuthorsGetPublished.com

Toronto, ON

Copyright © 2023 by Dr. Christine Topjian

All rights reserved. No part of this publication may be reproduced, distributed, or transmitted in any form or by any means, including photocopying, recording, or other electronic or mechanical methods, without the prior written permission of the publisher, except in the case of brief quotations embodied in critical reviews and certain other noncommercial uses permitted by copyright law.

A Note From the Author

Hi There! Thanks for picking up my book! I hope this book manages to inspire you, teach you, and cause you to grow in your relationship with God....and then, as a direct offshoot of that, will help you improve all the relationships around you, and especially, helps you find the right man for you, the one God intended for you.

Enjoy the read and I hope you will be open to all its messages.

Pre-Intro and Some Understandings

Before you start to read this book, I want to mention a few things just so that you are aware that I am speaking from a certain position and with some understandings in place:

- This book is written specifically for women which means that you will read "Ladies" and other ways to address women in this book. Men are, of course, also welcome to pick up this book and to learn from it but the book is addressed to all women.

- This book (and all of my books) has great reverence for God and so "He" is always referred to with a capital H. You will see "Him", "His" and "He" peppered throughout. That is on purpose.

- This book is not only for the Christian woman. It is for women in general because the idea is that ideally, all women are invited to come to know God, and to come into an active and loving relationship with God. We all (I include myself) need God and if we deny that truth, we are in for a world of difficulties that we will try (in vain) to handle all on our own. Why in vain? Because we were created to be in loving communion with God every day (not just on

Sundays) and to rely on Him for help. This means that we do what we can and then let Him do what He needs to do!

- Prayer (and I highly encourage you and everyone around you to pray) is a way to ask God to do things for you (yes, it is more than fine to ask Him to do so) and for others and it is a great (and very necessary) thing to do. Daily. Sometimes hourly.

- Prayer is absolutely essential because without it, we cannot thank God and we cannot make our requests known to God. There is no limit to what you can pray for. Pray deeply, pray for long periods of time, pray and pray and pray. Pray in your car and in the subway and on your way to work and before you meet your friends, and during your fitness time, and at any time you can.

- This book takes the factual, Scriptural position that God always wants to hear from you and I and the next person and that He loves it when we go to Him in prayer. With that, He sees that you are relying on Him and He loves that. We were never meant to do life on our own.

- Be specific in your prayers. God is a legalist and He takes into consideration each word you say in your prayers. So be more specific and state what you want specifically and then ask God if those things are also in His will for you. You can pray a number of things that you think you want but you won't know for sure until you get it. God, on the other hand, already knows you better than you know yourself so He is in a perfect position to tell you exactly where you will be happiest and which road is the right one for you to take. A lady I know prayed that she would "have the opportunity to love on these particular people" during their trip. Her prayer was answered: the people in question ended up in a huge accident and needed to spend days in the hospital while the lady I know was taking care of them - and this was during their vacation. That is clearly not the kind of "opportunity to love on them" that she intended but if you think about it, her prayer was answered and she had many opportunities to "love on them". So, in future, she can say "have the opportunity to love on them with everyone having a wonderful time and without anything bad happening to them or to me".

- If you are not sure what some of the words mean, please do look them up. You will get so much more out of this book if you do so. And I personally would like you to get maximum benefit out of this book. In fact, I'd like the people around you to also get maximum benefit from this book, which is why I enclose in the back a section called "pay it forward".

- Please do the reflections. There is space purposely left so that you can engage in the reflections and you can write them out meaningfully for yourself. When you take the time to engage in and do the reflections and you take the time to engage in the suggested prayers, you really do get so much more out of this book.

- This book takes the position that Jesus is the One true Son of God and is the Savior of the world. This means that He will also be referred to with a capital H and all prayers mentioned will be in His good name, followed by "Amen".

- This book takes the position that there are two genders: male and female, as created and dictated from birth by God.

- This book refers to the Bible and quotes the Bible as the unerring and infallible word of God, the One true Guide for life and the Book that contains the wisdom of God. We focus on the New Testament as Christ the Messiah has come and is the fulfillment of past prophecies.

- When it comes to the reflection spaces to giving the book to others for their learning, here is a suggestion in terms of how to use the space provided while giving your friend or family space as well: take a separate page to do your reflection or tear a part of the page out and do your reflection and then pass it to your friend or family. I'd like each person using the book to be sure that they are engaging in and doing the reflections so that we can make sure that these messages and its teachings benefit the maximum number of people.

- This book assumes that you may very well be interested in some prayers to help you achieve the best life that God has for you. As such, and like I mentioned before, some suggested prayers are offered. Of course, if you want to change or amend the prayer a little bit in an effort to have your prayer be more personalized and customized to what you feel God has put in your heart, then I encourage you to do so. But remember what I said: God is a legalist and every word you pray matters and will be factored in. Write the prayers out first if you can.

All the best blessings to you, dear reader!

Introduction

Just like there is a right guy out there for you, there is also a wrong guy. The wrong guy is the guy that God is telling you is not right for you. The wrong guy is the guy that you know isn't good to you or isn't good enough to you and that God is telling you to move away from. How is He telling you that? Listen carefully and closely because God is always talking. The question is: are you listening?

I want to mention here that we may not realize or understand fully that God is speaking to us. Many people, Christians included, don't realize that God is always talking to us and is always wanting us to realize the truth: the true value of a person, a person's true intent, the true value of a person, the true meaning behind the things they say and do, and more. Many of us may be tempted to go running off to our friends or family to discover the truth or to get their perspective - and that does have its place - but we must first go to God. How do we do that? Quite simply: we talk to Him as the loving Father that He is and we ask and then....we listen!

It could go a little something like this: "God, this is what is going on in my life right now. This is how I feel about it and this is my take on it. Illumine my mind. Show me the truth in this situation and tell me if I am missing something, if I am misunderstanding something....show me all that I need to see and know about this situation, please. In Jesus' mighty loving name. Amen"

And then....listen!

Listen carefully because He will answer you. He does each and every single time. He answers you and the person next to you and the other person too. God desires to have a loving, personal, go-to relationship with each person. In fact,

He longs for this and waits for you to decide that this is what you want too. So when you pray and ask Him for His guidance and His wisdom, listen after you pray and let Him talk to you.

Why the Wrong Guy Is the Wrong Guy

Why is that guy the wrong guy? Great question. Apart from the fact that there will always be signs and hints to demonstrate this, trusting in God and His answers is also where faith comes into play a little bit and where we need to have that faith that God is a God that knows best, knows us, created us and him and can tell us which man is the right man. He knows who you and he are today, who you both were and who you will both be many years from now. After all, in any relationship and marriage, the parties will evolve, will change, will develop and will have different personalities after some time. Even life events can change each person a little bit or a lot and that is going to be a new person, or for another way of saying it: a new version of themselves.

God factors all of these things in when He put him in your path and you in his. He factors in these things when He tells you that this man is right for you but not right now because he or you or he and you need to change a bit, grow as individuals, and then come back together as more mature and settled people. And these things will be figured out via conversations that may be a little bit difficult and may even sting a bit at first. We have to realize that while some of these conversations are difficult, they are necessary and we do have to be honest with our love interest. We have to be honest with the person because we cannot have a relationship with him without being honest about our true intentions, our true feelings, and our true words.

I was in this situation many years ago with a man I cared for and liked quite a bit. Because of my own fears, insecurities and listening to people around me who may or may not have had the best intentions toward me, I did not communicate what I really wanted and how I really felt about him and what I wanted with him. As a result, we ended up on a wheel going nowhere and with a relationship that was fraught with lies and with half-truths. It was in a word: stupid. This man came back into my life 20 years later and as he and I had both grown a lot as people, we were both able to be completely honest with each other. I was able to convey my true feelings to him, and I had the confidence to tell him what I really wanted. What a difference that made! He was able to maturely listen to and process and take my true feelings into account when we talked about things. He was able to respond to my actual feelings - not what other people told me I should be wanting and feeling.

The Diamond in the Rough

There are diamonds in the rough. Ladies, these are men who are good hearted and want and do treat you well but they need some time, some care and they need to soften their edges a little bit. A diamond in the rough can be any of the following:

- a guy who has never been in a relationship before and so he isn't sure what the right things are to say and do
- a guy who has never been given a chance at love before and so he is lost on how to show you his feelings
- a guy who has been hurt by someone and therefore isn't sure how to proceed in his next love quest
- a guy who was never taught how to treat a woman right (ex. hold her chair out for her, buy her flowers before a date..)
- a guy who is not very confident in himself for a variety of reasons and therefore needs you to be a little bit patient while he works on how to communicate his feelings
- a guy who has been "friend-zoned" by you and so he doesn't know how to express that he feels for you as more than a friend
- a guy who has stepped out in love before and he's been hurt so now he is gun-shy

All of the men in these scenarios are going to need a bit of help, time and understanding to make sure they are comfortable and can have open season opportunity to be your man.

Some Cases

Bob & Mindy: In the case of Bob who married Mindy. After 5 years of marriage, Mindy started to become a much more spiritual person and wanted to go to church regularly. This was something very different from how she was in the past and Bob, not being a spiritual person or a person of faith, was having a very hard time with this. His thought process was that he did not marry a person of faith because he himself was uncomfortable talking about that and so he was not ok with this new-found way his wife of 5 years had become. So, Bob (and Mindy) both had a choice to make about how they were going to proceed with things. They both had to decide what their individual and coupled future was going to look like and whether they were going to stay together and grow together or whether they were going to call it quits and decide that they would go their separate ways.

Marty & Joanne: In the case of Marty and Joanne, Marty had done the same work for 25 years and then decided that he wanted to change his career, he wanted to stop being a stockbroker and he wanted to pursue his dream of being a full-time painter. Well, this was going to change Marty: his ways, his personality, his routines and his income. Joanne had to make a decision about whether she was going to be on-board with the changes Bob had been wanting to make and then, whether she was going to support these changes in her husband.

A personal story:

If you have previously read my books, I have talked about a man from my past that upon realizing my romantic interest in him, I prayed to God about him to see if he was the right person for me. I found out fairly quickly that in fact, he was not. Needless to say, I was very disappointed because I had found myself to have feelings for him and I wanted the answer to be: "Yes! He is it! Go forward!"

But alas, that was not the answer. The answer was that he was meant for someone else and that I needed to deal with that by understanding God's will (and how His will is more important and wiser than my own), by praying to understand who was the right person for me and by setting my sights on another worthwhile person for me.

One of the most important points I need to make in this book is the following: ask God. I'll repeat it because it is so important:

> Ladies, ask God! And then listen to hear His response. The response may be audible words, nudgings, strong feelings and more...but....listen and pay attention!

So now that we know that we need to ask God who the right guy is for you and that we need to pay attention to hear Him, the following are some follow-up questions we need to ask:

- Where your right man is?
- What is he doing?
- Is he currently working on himself?
- Is he a man of faith?
- What can God tell you about him?
- Is he someone already in your life?
- How can you pray for him from now?
- What are some things that are really important to him?
- What are some of his qualities and traits that make him the right person for me?

> Let God be the Author of your romance.

A Revolutionary Approach

This approach of asking God who the right man is for you is pretty revolutionary. Why? Because not many people do this and not many people know to do this. Not many people take the time to pray about whether the person they are interested in, seeing or in a relationship with is actually the person meant to be with them and for them. The only person who can give that answer is God Himself. Not many people ask God (or even have that relationship with God) where they feel ok enough or comfortable enough to ask Him who the right person is for them.

Many people just go online or ask friends and family to set them up or some version of this. Now don't get me wrong: that could be the right way God chooses for you to meet that person (sure, why not!) but let God be the Author of your romance. Let God be the One who tells you:

- who he is
- where he is
- your current role in his life
- what he is doing
- his emotional state
- his psychological state
- how you will come together
- who his family is
- how you can start praying for him from now

I also want to make this really clear: even if you are not yet a believer in God, you CAN still go to Him. You CAN still use this process and you CAN still approach God and He will answer you. You have to remember that while you may not know God yet, He knows you very well. He loves you, created you and knows every hair that is on your head. So if you have never spent 5 minutes with Him before or it's been a while since you've last talked to Him, you CAN and SHOULD still go to Him and talk to Him.

Don't Take It Into Your Own Hands

This section encourages you to not take the matter into your own hands and by that I mean that don't take on the stance that you saw this guy and you're impressed with him for such-and-such reason and so you have decided that he is "it". That would be an unwise approach. You need to ask God who he is, if he is right for you and if this is the right timing for you two.

You see, reader, whether you are an active Christian or not, this concept applies to you: God loves you so much and He wants you to have that happiness and that blessing of being with the right person. He knows that just like there is a right person for you, there is also a wrong person for you and nobody knows that better than Him. Nobody also knows better than Him that the wrong person can come into your life masquerading as the right person, and that will eventually be detrimental to your life.

Many people today often say for you to choose…be the author of your own destiny. I don't agree with that. We were always meant to go to God to get our answers and to rely on His Godly wisdom, not on our own human understanding.

> (Proverbs 3:5-6) Trust in the Lord with all your heart and lean not on your own understanding; in all your ways submit to him, and he will make your paths straight.

When Scripture says that He will make your paths straight, what it is saying is that God will make the way clear and unencumbered so that you can access His best for you. We all know that in love, we can often meet many many roadblocks. As such, having God in our corner as the One who can eliminate or help us break down those roadblocks in the ways that are needed would be a tremendous help! Wouldn't you like God to help you through the difficulties you are experiencing, no matter what stage in the process you are in? I know I did and still would.

So, why not take the smart route and get to be with the right guy, right as defined by God? That may very well require you to get over and get past the wrong guy. You can think of this book as your go-to manual to really understand how to get past the wrong guy and how to make sure you understand your next steps to success with the right guy.

Let's dive right in!

1

The Good Wrong Guy

There is such a thing as the good wrong guy.

Who is the good wrong guy?

He is the guy who is a good guy and treats you well and may even be a great guy but he isn't the right person for you. As hard as it may be to hear it, he isn't meant for you but rather, for another lady. That means that there is someone else "out there" for you.

Case in point: A lady named Eliana and her relationship with Robert are a perfect example of this. Eliana is a very sweet girl and was looking for love when a friend set her up with Robert (who is a really sweet guy and was also looking for love). Eliana and Robert met and began dating and seemed to like each other but one could see that they were extremely ill-suited to each other. Robert wanted certain things in life while Eliana wanted very different things and one could see that they were great friends, not romantic partners. Robert was nice, well-educated with a very good head on his shoulders but that doesn't make him the right man for just anyone. Eliana's friends were also telling her that while Robert was a good guy, but that they didn't seem to be compatible in the long-term sense. Robert has a woman out there who is the right person for him and will fit him in a much better way. Eliana, of course, also has a right person for her and is encouraged to tap into whom that may be by asking God about him and praying for God to bring her that man.

If you are a woman who picked up this book and you are with a good wrong guy or you suspect that the man you are with might be, pray about it to receive confirmation from God. When you have taken some time to mull this over and you feel confident in the response, take comfort in the fact that like I mention earlier in the book, there is a right man for you. It just might not be the person you are currently with or that you are currently dating or interested in.

If you need to let the guy down, there are very kind and respectful ways to do that.

While breakups can definitely be unpleasant and people often would rather just send a text to break things off or even avoid the person altogether by ghosting them, this is not something I would suggest you do. There is a benefit in breaking things off with the person in the right way that is respectful, kind and that helps the person know that while you appreciated your time with them and all you have shared together, that your time together has come to an end and that you will need to move on and he should too. There is always a classy and a crass way of doing these things. Even if you are going to be delivering bad news to him, doing it in a kind and respectful way is likely to cause him to look back on your time together with fondness even though you two weren't meant to be.

The good wrong guy is the guy whom many may automatically think is the right person for you because he is a kind, well-spoken and an all-around good guy. But again, just because he is these things, it doesn't make him right for you. A lady I know whom I will name Bernice fell into this trap. She had met a guy online and they began dating and he was definitely a good wrong guy. Bernice shared with me that she knew that this was not the right man but she persisted to date him because he was so nice. In fact, she dated him years because he was the first good guy she had ever dated. I completely understand the desire to stay with a good guy but it would not ultimately serve you both to continue with the relationship, if your goal is to be married. Bernice also began to see that in the long-term, they were not right for each other but rather than let him go, she married him. Bernice shared that she had gotten married because she wanted the white picket fence life and she thought that because this man could provide that, that she should just marry him. A few months into an unhappy marriage, Bernice admitted that she had made a mistake in marrying him.

A Great Guy Is....Great! But....

Ladies, a great guy is great. They should be celebrated and appreciated. However, your job is to find the right one for you based on what God tells you, not based on what the world tells you. I will qualify that point some more: the world may say to be with someone who has lots of money and can give you the things you want. That's not necessarily the man God wants you to be with. Very often (and I say this with all due respect to the well-intentioned friends you may have), our friends and people around us haven't prayed and haven't begun to seek God's wisdom in what they are doing or for what you are doing. They haven't begun to seek God's answers on whether the guy they are with is right for them or whether the guy you are seeing is right for you. Many do not factor this in but it is essential that they begin doing so.

Uncertainty

There is nothing wrong with being uncertain about a guy.

You may be in the process of trying to figure out the suitability of a certain man and you may be in the process of collecting as much info as possible or trying to hear from God clearly. There is nothing wrong with being uncertain about a guy. What I do suggest is letting God help you with that important process and to see what He says about that certain guy and his suitability for you and then following-through on it. You may initially not like the answer you get, and you may need to take some time to let it ruminate but ultimately, I hope that you will come to see that God's take on it is right. After all, He created both of you and He knows exactly who is the right good guy for you and who is the right woman for him.

I also want to note that when people are in the process of trying to decide, they may feel a little bit confused and/or a little bit worried. These emotions are normal and ok. Do not beat yourself up over feeling this way because it makes sense to feel that way while you are trying to figure this out. These are really important matters and rushing into anything is not a good idea. So take your time and feel good and feel confident with your decision. You are going to have to live with this decision for the rest of your life - wouldn't it make sense, then, to trust this decision to the One who knows you the best and knows him and is the Father of all wisdom, who understands and knows each of your days and what will make you ultimately happy?

The Wrong Decision = PROBLEM!

I hope I don't come off as harsh when I say this but if you are making the wrong decision and you are going with a guy who is contrary to what God has told you, there will be problems and with problems comes a fair bit of suffering. God tries to avoid unnecessary suffering for us because He loves us so much and so when we don't heed His warnings and we don't do what He is saying, we are going to run into lots of problems and maybe possibly an inevitable divorce.

Think about it: how can you have a solid and sustainable marriage with the wrong guy? Marriage takes a lot of:
* work
* time
* commitment
* love
* understanding
* compromise and putting the other person's feelings ahead of your own

Marriage was always meant to include three parties: the man, the woman and God. God is supposed to be there to help you through your marriage. He is supposed to help you both with compromising, loving each other, putting the other person first, understanding and much more. So if you are finding it difficult to get these things done, there is a reason. Neither you nor your spouse is supposed to handle these things all on your own! Ask God to help you, to give you the strength and to help you through all that you are going through. Even if it is just asking Him to give you perspective and some help, ask Him to do that because that can make such a difference in both of your lives.

How Does This Relate to the Wrong Guy?

So....how does this relate to getting over the good wrong guy? Simple. You will need to rely on God to help you through that. If the guy is not the right person for you (or not the right person right now) then you can (and should) ask God to help you move past him. He will. You will start to notice that each day, things will get a little easier, a little less hard, a little bit more manageable. That is God helping you through. That is God helping you heal and deal with the pain of letting someone go.

Here is a prayer you can pray to help you through this: *"God, I am going to ask You to help me. Help me heal and help me move on from this man. Help make this less difficult to go through because I am having a hard time with it. You know the exact intricacies of the situation and You know better than anyone what I need and what I am going through. I am asking You for Your help. I am asking You to help me through each step of this and to help me get over him. I know that You are aware of the situation in its entirety....please help me get through this and get me to the other side where I can feel good and feel happy and fulfilled again. In Jesus' name. Amen."*

2

Chin Up

When we go through difficult things, as we all do at some point or other in life, we need to do our best to keep things in perspective that we are now free to move on and to love someone else.

Every person will go through many trials in life and face many difficulties from time to time. That's just part of life. When we take the time to remember that this trial is making us stronger if we allow it to, and if we stay mindful that we can use our pain to maybe help someone else out who may be going through something similar someday, then we can actually learn a great deal from this situation and things begin to look very different. You begin to look at things from a hopeful standpoint instead of one where you may be feeling hopeless.

Some of the greatest (and strongest) people I know or have had the pleasure to come across are people who have been through great trials but still manage to keep their chins up, still manage to have a good and kind attitude and demeanor, and still manage to put their best into their work, their families and into others by being a help while they were or are in their own time of difficulty. We really do get a great feeling of happiness and satisfaction when we are there for others when they are in pain or in need, and it can really help lift us out of how we are feeling at the moment.

Some people wonder "why does heartbreak hurt so much?" The simple truth is that it hurts because it is the loss of something we thought was going to be happening for us. It is the loss of a possibility that we thought was going to make us happy and it is the realization that this person is not going to be "that person" in our lives but rather, that he is meant to be "that person" in someone else's life. I recall very vividly that when I had the realization (after some time of quiet contemplation) that the object of my affections at the time was not going to be "my person" but that he would instead be someone else's. Initially, it made me feel a bit sick and queasy. It took me a good amount of prayer and time to get perspective to realize and to see that that was a good thing because it would not only bring someone I cared about happiness but that it was God's will and so I was happy that God's will was being done.

You see, dear reader, when you get to a point where you understand that God also has a heart, He has feelings and He can also get hurt by the many things that we humans do that are contrary to His will and contrary to our best interests, God's heart also breaks. In other words, when we make a decision that is against our best interests (ex. self-harming, falling into a cult, considering or committing suicide, taking drugs, speaking negatively over ourselves, etc.), God's heart breaks because He loves us so much and only wants the very best for us. Sometimes that will mean disciplining us because He loves us, not because He wants to be a mean God. Disciplining us is His way of showing us He loves us because He is trying to teach us exactly the way good parents teach their children the right ways through discipline and through consequences for wrong ways taken after being taught what is right.

Knowing that, it also stands to reason (and this helped to make me feel a lot better when I had my heartbreak) that because He wants the best for each and every one of us, that He will also bring me the best person for me. This means that the one I had my eye on was not the best option for me. There was someone else better and writing this years after that experience, I now have the benefit of hindsight where I can really say that my current happiness is on and with someone else, someone I feel is much better suited to me and to my personality.

He Is Working On You….And On Him

When God has you single for a time, it is not time wasted. God doesn't waste time when He plans things out for you and presents you with an open door. When God has you single for a time, it is because He is going to bring you the right person but He is giving you time to work on yourself with Him, to develop yourself with Him, and to work on your relationship with Him. This means that He is giving you time to develop all of the following:

- Patience
- Perspective
- A closer relationship with Him
- Understanding
- Maybe develop your career

- Right some wrongs from the past
- Spend time meaningfully as a single person with people currently around you
- Enjoy the time you have now where you can do whatever you would like
- Understand what being married really involves
- Learning to compromise and all the tenets that are involved in healthy & happy marriages

All are very worthwhile and very important endeavors.

A Great Relationship With You

Having a great relationship with yourself means that you are good to yourself, you are kind to yourself, that you love yourself and that you love spending time with yourself. When we take the time to include God in the equation, to spend time with Him and to get to know who He really is and to develop that relationship with Him, we get access to the greatest wisdom that is available.

In an effort to help you gauge your relationship with yourself and your next steps in this journey, I will ask you these questions. Feel free to jot down the answers in the space provided:

1. How much time do you spend with yourself?
   _____
2. How much time do you enjoy spending with yourself?
   _____

3. How much time do you spend with God?
   _____

4. How much time do you spend praying to God?
   _____

5. Do you spend time working on yourself and improving yourself through books, hobbies and more?
   _____

6. Do you spend time in quiet prayer and meditation each day?
   _____

7. Do you spend time reading and understanding the Bible?
   _____

8. Do you enjoy spending time alone with and journaling with God? _____

9. How much time have you spent asking God where and what your calling is?
   _____

Time with God....It's Invaluable!

Spending time with God might seem like a foreign concept to you or one you have never heard of before but it doesn't have to be. The quiet time we spend with God is so important and so precious. It is truly a time where we can connect with the One who loves us the most - more than we love ourselves, more than our parents or guardians love us, more than any person could love us. Don't forget that God is a Spirit and a Supernatural God which means that no human can love us the way that God loves us. Therefore, when you spend time with Him, know that you are spending time with the person who loves you the most and wants to talk to you the most.

A lady I met many years ago in a Bible study class said it this way and I simply loved it because it echoed my own experience to be true. She said "I have a very personal and loving relationship with God and it is my own, unlike any other relationship that I have." With each person, God cultivates His own personal and private relationship and He loves to do so. Your relationship with Him is going to be personal to you and if you don't have one yet, invite Him into your life today. Here is a suggested prayer if you would like to call God into your life today. Remember that God can read your mind and your thoughts, so you do not need to say the prayer out loud. You can say it in your mind and He will hear you. *God, I want to have a close, personal relationship with You. This is important to me and I would like to ask You to come into my life and to show me what a close, personal relationship with You looks like. Please make it clear and obvious to me what this will look like. In Jesus' name. Amen.*

> When you spend time with God, you are not only spending time with the One who loves you the most but you are also spending time building yourself up and building up your self-esteem and your sense of self-worth because when we know our Maker, we begin to realize why (and the importance) of why we were made, and that's something I feel confident enough in saying that everyone wants to know.

And spending time with God can mean the most lovely of quiet time and enjoyment. You can take a walk in the park and talk to God and that counts as time spent. God is also the Author of laughter and of fun so you can actually go and spend time watching a comedy movie and still have that time with Him. One of the most important concepts of this book is the following: when you spend time with God, you are not only spending time with the One who loves you the most but you are also spending time building yourself up and building up your self-esteem and your sense of self-worth because when we know our Maker, we begin to realize why (and the importance) of why we were made, and that's something I believe everyone wants to know about.

Your Time Is SO Valuable

Your time is valuable - that is a simple fact. When you spend time with the wrong guy, then you are wasting your time a little bit. When you spend a lot of time with the wrong guy, then you are wasting your time quite a lot. And you don't need to.

When we have that close relationship with God, we cut out the unnecessary. We cut out time with the wrong person that we are not supposed to be having and He helps us to see that. Please know that the words that I am writing in the pages of this book are words that I write because of lots of time spent alone with God but also, because of lots of time spent pondering the experiences I have had that He guided me to have and that I have learned and grown from.

Speaking of valuable time, I will take the example of a lady I know I will name Laura. Laura had been in a relationship with Jay for almost ten years. They had started dating at a fairly young age and had been together ever since. Their friends began seeing them as a package deal and Laura seemed really happy. I knew Laura socially through friends so when Jay finally proposed and they were engaged, I heard about it pretty quickly. What I also heard about pretty quickly is that Jay was acting strangely during wedding planning and there were rumblings of concern about whether the wedding was even going to happen. In the end, Laura and Jay did get married but from the wedding day, friends and family could see that Jay was not behaving as a man who had just gotten married and that Laura was starting to look quite unhappy. Laura's friends and family began asking some questions about Jay's appropriateness at the wedding and about what was really going on behind the scenes. Laura felt crushed but she was such a gentle soul that she opted to keep her mouth shut when people were trying to probe and ask questions. Ultimately, just a few months after they had gotten married, Jay decided to break things off and abruptly moved out of the home they shared and had moved into as a married couple, promptly requesting a dissolution of marriage and making it clear that he wasn't going to take no for an answer from Laura or from anyone else.

It took Laura many months of counseling and therapy to begin to understand just what had happened and why it had happened. She spent months in counseling trying to understand that she had missed or ignored the many, many warning signs over the years, including Jay's secrecy, his lack of respect toward her on many occasions, and that he had many times in the past hesitated to move things forward in commitment to her. She began to see how Jay was not the right man for her and that listening to her family and friends who encouraged her to move things forward with him was ultimately not the right way to go. I believe strongly that if Laura had taken the time to pray and to seek God's will in the situation, that she would not have ended up in that specific situation and could possibly have saved herself a fair bit of heartache and time.

> This means that you will have to pray about this because there is no better person to go to than the One who should be the author of your love story.

Ladies, don't waste time with the person you know, you sense, and that God tells you is the wrong person. You do deserve God's very best for you and God (not your friends or family) should be the very first person you go to with the question of "Is he the right man for me?"

Yes, this means that you will have to pray about this because there is no better person to go to than the One who should be the Author of your love story.

3

Activating Through Prayer

This chapter is about activating God's goodness and answers into your life through the blessing of prayer. This chapter provides suggested prayers and how to hear from God so you can get your answer about whether the man in question is the right person for you.

For the reasons I mention in previous chapters, we would be very wise to go to God and ask Him in prayer if the man in question is the right person for us. You can go to Him in prayer at church, in your room alone, at a chapel, while sitting in the park, etc. It matters much less how you do this so long as you do it.

Here are a couple of sample prayers you can pray for this (of course, you can change some of the words to best suit your situation and/or how you feel):

Father God, I come to You in prayer so that You can reveal to me who the right man for me is. You know my current situation and the person I am with or the person who is the object of my affections. I am coming to You and asking You to lead me to understanding whether this person is the right person for me or whether they are not. If they are not, please lead me and put in my mind the right person.

Another suggested prayer:

God, I need Your help. I am understanding that just as there is a right man for me, there is or are also wrong men. I am coming to You to ask You to help me decipher who is the right person for me. I need You to be very clear about this and to tell me clearly and directly who the right person is and do so in a way that will make it unmistakably evident to me. Speak to my heart in a way that only you can. In Jesus' name. Amen

These prayers are asking God to speak to you and to reveal His will to you. They are powerful. Then, we have to pay attention and see what the response will be.

Christine, Why Do I Have To "Activate"?

We need to "activate" because God appreciates being asked. He invites us to ask Him when we are in need of something. In

Scripture, you will see that when a person wants something, they go to God in prayer. Even Jesus did this many times throughout Scripture and all people in Scripture went ahead and made sure they prayed and asked God to bring them certain things. These are what we call activation prayers because they activate God to work something out on our behalf.

To be clear, God can act on His own. He can do anything He wants. He appreciates and invites us to go to Him in prayer so that He can see that we are relying on and depending on Him. He invites us to pray to Him about everything and anything because that way He can see that we are relying on Him and on His provision. So God does get happy when we pray to Him because He can see that we are relying on Him!

> Matthew 7:7 "Ask and it will be given to you; seek and you will find; knock and the door will be opened to you.

God has given us the gift of being able to pray so that you have the option and can make the choice of going to Him in prayer and asking Him to step in and to help you with anything. He is waiting for you to ask Him and because we all have free will, He wants to see that you are choosing to go to Him and then when He reveals His answers to you, He is waiting to see that you will choose to honor and obey what He is saying. Everything we do is a choice and so when we pray and God speaks to us, He is looking to see if you will choose to follow Him and listen to Him or if you will choose to go your own way.

Yes, I have included the word choose a few times in this chapter and that is by design. I state again that we have all been given free will (which is why we can select to do whatever we want), and which means that we have to choose the way that we will take. Will you take your own way based on your own human and self understanding or will you choose to go His way and let Him guide you to His choices for your best life? God is letting you (giving you the opportunity) choose the way that you will go. You can go to Him or you can not go to Him. It is your choice and you will reap the benefits if you choose well just as you will face consequences (time wasted, running into bad situations, etc) if you go your own way after having asked but gone your own way instead or not asking Him at all. It is, in the end, all your choice.

To help you understand the importance of following-through on what God guides you to do, I will use an example from my own life. I chose to go the way that I saw best after I prayed to God for how I should handle something. God warned me about a man whom I would develop an interest in, named Trevor. When I met Trevor, he seemed great. Kind, considerate, very cute and seemed to have a great head on his shoulders. Despite God's warnings, I promptly started spending more and more time with Trevor and promptly started to really like him. I liked him so much that I started to do things that were out of character for me and put myself in some less-than-desirable situations. I decided to ignore the people around me who were warning me that things didn't seem right and decided that they simply didn't know how I felt. As time wore on and Trevor and I hung out together more, I began to notice actions on his part that were downright disrespectful - comments, actions and more that were putting me down a little bit. He was also starting to make it clear that he was only interested in a sexual tryst.

This continued for a few weeks and more and more I liked Trevor until one day, he promptly began ghosting me (this is the process some men take when they are letting a woman know they are not interested and so they start to avoid her texts, her calls, etc.) The part that hit the hardest was finding out that he had actually gotten engaged to a girl he had gotten to know a few weeks prior. So while I was developing a deeper interest in him, he had already met and had moved on with another girl. I remember the numbness I felt in my body when I found out about this and how I tried to cover it up (with little success) from the people around me. I gratefully recall the look of genuine empathy one friend gave me when she read correctly past the mask I had on, stating that I was "just fine" but she could see that I had been crumbling on the inside.

That's what happens when you choose to ignore God's warning signs and you choose to follow your own wisdom. It took me a little while to recover from all of that and to reconnect with God (not to mention learn from the experience so that I don't repeat it again) and fortunately with lots of time spent on myself, time in fitness and reflection, I could see where I had gone wrong and healed well from the entire situation. I include this example at this point in the book so that you can benefit from my experience and you can not make the same mistake as me.

I also learned from there that the heartache is not always necessary to go through and that God was trying to lovingly prevent me from experiencing that.

Think back for a moment to a time or two when you may have sensed that God was trying to guide you to or away for something and if you listened to Him. If you did not listen to Him, why not?

If you had to do that part over again, would your response be the same?

Praying for Wisdom

Can we pray for wisdom?

We certainly can and we certainly should. Asking God for wisdom is a great way to accomplish all of the following:

- Shows respect and reverence for God
- Shows that you respect His word and what He is guiding you to
- Shows that you are smart enough to not rely on your own human understanding because you know that there is always more to a situation than meets the eye
- Show that you want His perspective and not relying on just your own
- A great way to make sure that you are asking God for what is the bigger picture

When we pray for wisdom, let's be prepared to receive it. Let's open ourselves up to new ways of thinking of things, to new perspectives and to having a greater and deeper respect for God's word. How are they related? Very simply. When we pray for wisdom, we understand that we will need to consider things in a different way and we understand that people, our understanding, situations and contexts may very well be different than how we thought they were.

For example, when Carmen was considering whether to move in with her boyfriend, she knew that her upbringing didn't really support that. She knew that living together without being married was living in sin. She prayed about it so that she could get perspective on it and not just rely on her own understanding. Pretty soon, Carmen began attending a Bible study that she felt led to attend and began to understand why living together would not be a good idea. She realized that not only would that qualify as entering into a deep sin but that it wasn't God's will and seeing the example of Adam and Eve as well as all the women of the Bible who ended up with their right man, she took it a step further and asked whether this man was the right man for her. Carmen's answer came quickly and swiftly. There was no mistaking that this man was not God's will for her and she prayed to have the conviction to break things off with him in a clean and respectful manner.

Here is a suggested prayer to ask for wisdom in this area:

Father God, I am coming to You, asking for wisdom. I need wisdom in this very important area of my life and I am asking You to help me figure this out. I need Your wisdom in understanding what is going on and in deciphering what is Your will in all that I am doing and in what is coming and then, for what I should do with it. I need to know based on Your wisdom and to not rely on my own understanding. You know peoples' hearts and You know their motivations. Help me see the truth in each situation. In Jesus' name, I pray. Amen.

When you pray this simple but strong prayer, be prepared to receive your answers. Be prepared to receive a superior understanding and to see things not for how they may seem, but as they really are.

The answers she received (in the example just before the prayer) were, like I said, swift and decisive. He was not the right person and moving in with him would have cost her time, hurt her heart and in the end, would have been totally contrary to God's best will for her life. She realized in quiet meditation and reflection that from the beginning, her boyfriend had been guiding her away from God and away from the Christian teachings she had received since a young age. It began to be really clear to her that this was not the man for her and that he had many of his own issues to work on. She began to see how praying for wisdom and perspective totally changed her outlook and how it saved her in so many ways. Carmen still attends Bible study and very much enjoys the time she is spending with God to grow into the person He intends for her to be. Instead of falling into sin, she fell into a glorious relationship with God.

4

Feelings Are Fickle and Fleeting

I hope this chapter title does not come off as insensitive but the fact is: feelings are fickle and they can be fleeting. We can feel strongly or very strongly about one thing or one person today but eventually, we can feel completely differently in a few weeks, months or years. We cannot rely on just our feelings to tell us where we are going and whether this person is the right one for us.

> Many women often feel that because they feel one way about something, that they will always feel that way about it. That is simply not true.

We also have to pray about our feelings and ask for wisdom and for clarity because feelings can be from God and they can also not be from God. The enemy would love to make you think you are totally head over heels for the wrong guy because then, you will be distracted and not pursue God's best for you.

Many women often feel that because they feel one way about something, that they will always feel that way about it. That is simply not true. You can feel really good about someone at one point in your life but then things can change, circumstances can change and so can your feelings. This is why it is possible to get over the wrong person and to move on to greater and stronger feelings for the right person.

This is also a great place in the book to point out that you may not be interested in the right guy when you meet him. Maybe he doesn't look the way you think your man should look or doesn't behave the way you think your man should….but there is great wisdom in following God's leading if he is the right guy and in giving yourself time to really get to know the guy and to seeing that maybe he had a bit of a rough exterior but he is really great. Sometimes a great guy who is the right person for you needs some help and some guidance on how to show his love and his care for you in a way that you would actually like.

A male friend of mine from years ago jumped on this point when I made it in a conversation. He pointed out very quickly that "how am I supposed to know what to do to let a girl know I like her when I have never been shown how to do that?" He continued saying "I want to show her I like her in the way that she desires but I don't know the right way (or the right words) to use to do that." I felt a lot of empathy for him and respected him for putting it just like that. It was a very honest sentiment and I think more guys feel that way than not. I helped him construct his words and his approach for the girl of his desires and if you have a friend like that who expresses the like, I hope that you too will help him or her.

Humans Are Adaptable

Humans are adaptable. They can change and they can grow and they can learn. They can develop and when they do, great changes can occur. If we were to listen to only our feelings all the time, then we will likely be living a fickle and fairly unstable life. We cannot and we should not rely on our own understanding because we are not always given the full truth - people can lie to us, people can tell us half-truths, people can do and say many things that may lead us to believe one thing that may not be the truth.

It's like if we don't feel like going to work in the morning. We can feel that way and we may not go to work one morning but we can't keep that up if we want to keep that job. We need to show up for work just like we need to show up for life. Our life.

> We have to be very careful about the source of our feelings. They can be from God and they can not be from God.

Feelings, Feelings, Feelings

Feelings can come from God and they can also come from darkness. Darkness can also cause us to think we have feelings for someone, and I can guarantee you that darkness will never guide you to God's right person for you.

Darkness will guide you to the relationship that makes you fall into confusion, uncertainty, sin and difficulty. One way that darkness does this is by providing you with any option other than the right one. I recall when I was being deceived in this way and I met what I thought was a great guy. I began dating him and I actually really liked him and he made sure to show me the good sides of himself (which is not abnormal in dating). But, what I began to realize after two plus years of dating him is that he was not just showing me the good sides of himself but he was outright deceiving me and manipulating me. This became apparent to me when I discovered that had been cheating on me and with me as well (that too was part of the learning process I went through) and many friends who knew him confirmed for me that he had himself admitted to cheating on me. It also, in hindsight, became clear to me that he and his family were doing their best to lead me away from Christ - they began presenting me with spiritual options other than Christ. And I fell for it for some time. It took me some time to put all of this together and to realize that I had gotten involved with a wrong relationship and that I needed to get out. This was many years ago and in hindsight, I am extremely grateful that I saw the truth before I married him or made greater commitments to him. Today, I see that he continues to unfortunately make wrong choices when it comes to his marriage.

This therefore means that we have to be very careful about the source of our feelings and most importantly, we need to cultivate that close, personal bond with God so that when we meet someone or we have our eye on someone, we can ask Him whether this person is the right person for us or the wrong person. We are only human so we are not meant to have all of these answers on our own. We are supposed to be relying on God to show us, to help us, to lead us in the right ways.

How To Ask God

If you are a person who does have that relationship with God - a relationship where you know you can ask Him questions and you can get a sense of His response back to you - then I suggest you begin to cultivate that relationship today. Ask Him what you should do about something and listen carefully for His answers because He will answer.

If you are not a person who has that relationship with God, this same way to ask does apply to you too but what will be different is that people who don't know God yet will have to really understand that not only can you ask God questions but I am also letting you know that He will speak to you and will get His reply to you.

If this is new learning for you, take a moment and jot down this new learning because you can (and should, hopefully) be using it again and again and again in your life.

I am also including a section on some frequently asked questions on this topic at the end of this chapter that may be of assistance to you as you navigate this new realm or this new option you have (for free) at your fingertips 24 hours a day, 7 days a week because God is always available, always wants to hear from you, always wants to talk to you and always has your very best interests in mind and at heart. He also knows other people, their personalities, their ways, their desires, their level of faith, their true motives and more. He understands and knows the situation (every situation) in a way that you and I simply do not and so when He guides, He guides in ways that you and I may not completely understand right away but that's also because we don't have His amazing, 360 degree perspective.

Let's take Clive's example. Clive is a fine young man who was looking to get married to his girlfriend. Clive had been dating Betty for about 2 years and he felt that everything was on the up and up, that she had been honest and straight-forward with him and that everything was moving along swimmingly. When he prayed about marrying Betty, though, he instantly felt uneasiness. Something was not right about the situation but he didn't understand why. Finally, as he was on the precipice of making the very important (and very expensive decision) to buy the engagement ring or to not buy it, he cried out to God and asked God to explain to him why He was getting terrible responses to the prospect of marrying Betty.

Clive had asked and God was about to answer.

Clive was visited by the police 3 nights later. Clive was completely taken aback and did not understand why the police wanted to talk to him. In their conversation, the truth came out - that Betty had been working as a sex worker and that for almost two years, had not shared this information with Clive. Betty had been extremely dishonest with him and had been going behind his back with this work she had been doing but not only that, because Betty had had many partners, she had put Clive seriously at-risk of all kinds of illnesses that she may have picked up from her sexual partners.

Clive understood why he was getting such terrible feelings about proposing to her.

> So, how do we ask God about who the right guy is, and how do we ask God how to move past the wrong guy?

Keep In Mind

We must choose our words carefully when we ask God in prayer. Here are a couple of examples that I have provided for you:

> God, I am coming to You to ask for Your help. Will You please tell me who is the right guy for me?

> God, I am coming to You to ask for Your help. Will You please guide me and give me Your best answer about how to move on from _____.

Then, listen carefully.

God speaks to us in all of the following ways:

- Nudging and sensations
- Audible words if we are listening carefully
- Impressions
- People coming to us "coincidentally" with solutions
- Sermons that come our way
- Dreams
- Daydreams
- When during a sermon, you feel like the Holy Spirit is speaking to you directly
- Reading the Bible and feeling like a passage or sections are speaking to you
- Talking to a priest or a pastor and then praying over things with you and for you
- Reading Christian books that teach on these things

This is also why it is important to listen and to pay careful attention. Be mindful. When God speaks, it is not always with a booming and great big voice. It can also just be by whispers and nudging, so that is why we have to pay close attention to all that is going on, all that we may be feeling and sensing and to little hints that come our way.

Reading Christian Books

One of the most important things we can do is to read Christian books by Christian authors. I speak from personal experience when I say this because since I was a baby in Christ, just beginning to learn and to understand how to navigate the Bible, my relationship with Christ and so on, I was guided to read many Christian books which taught me such important lessons such as how to hear from God in audible ways, how to not rely on my own understanding, understanding God's personality and the way in which He operates, learning and knowing how to pray and much more. I learned from such wonderful Bible-based teachers and I began to realize that even though I felt that I had some understanding of who God is, I was only just beginning to scratch the tip of the topic. I had much to learn and the topic was fascinating. I appreciated every bit of wisdom (because that's what each of these Bible teachers provided) that came my way and that taught me something new that I was not aware of. Each shared their personal stories, testimonials, and experiences that taught me and that showed me the amazing and beautiful ways that God worked in their lives. I really felt and believed that if God had worked in that way in their lives, that He would in mine too.

You see, many people erroneously believe that God only gives wonderful gifts and favors to those who are pastors, preachers and the like. Some people have actually said to me "I have never had a relationship with God therefore God doesn't care about me." This kind of thinking is a lie. God loves each person and longs for you to go to Him. He loves you and only wants the best for you. No matter who you are, where you are from, what kind of background you come from and more, God loves you, wants a personal relationship with you and only ever wants the best for you. I hope that that lesson has been made clear in this chapter.

Your Feelings

One of the most important "tells" that you will have is your feelings and like I said earlier, asking God if the feelings you are feeling come from Him. When you feel strongly about someone, and God confirms to our hearts that those feelings are from Him, it is a pretty good indication that there is something happening here that we need to take a closer look at. We need to be really careful that we let the light of God in. To explain further, darkness wants all of the following for us:

- Confusion
- Chaos
- Misunderstanding
- Uncertainty
- Anger
- To act on our anger
- To harbor ill feelings
- To not talk about our true feelings
- To stay in chaos and confusion when it does happen
- To panic
- To worry
- To want to blame God for all that is wrong in the world
- To blame the actions (and misactions) of clergy members on God

Darkness knows that people want happiness and goodness, not unhappiness, problems and chaos, and so darkness masquerades as light.

> 2 Corinthians 11:14 "And it is no wonder. Even Satan tries to make himself look like an angel of light."

Knowing this, we have to be careful what we accept as fact and truth from God and understand how to know the difference between the light and the darkness. Darkness will specifically lead you to hurt, pain, abuse, unhappiness, confusion and will make you think that that is what you deserve. Let me be clear: that is not what you deserve and in a book about how to get over him, I would be remiss if I did not tell you that it is very important to consider what you think is from the light very carefully.

Here are some examples to help you better understand this very important concept:

Example 1: Janey had prayed aloud that God would bring her the right man after her breakup with Guaro, her boyfriend of over four years. Janey had felt very strongly that Guaro was not the right man for her, according to her prayers. When Janey prayed, she prayed out loud and she asked God to bring her the right man. Along came Jamie. Jamie seemed great on the surface but he was a man who, when he and Janey would fight, would hit her. A man from God will not be a man who abuses you or hits you so even though she had prayed for the right man to come, Jamie wasn't it so he was not the answer to her prayers. Wisdom states that Janey needed to continue to pray so that God actually brought her the right man.

Example 2: Roxanne had believed that her friend Roy could be the one that she had been considering for the rest of her life. She wondered if the right man would be one who would continually string her along and even sleep with her while still calling her "just a friend". Roxanne understood that Roy was not serious about her and in fact, would not commit to her. She came to understand that the right man would not do that to her but instead, would respect her and would be good unto her, honoring her and making her his wife, not just a play thing. You see, Roxanne incorrectly thought that because Roy was a friend, that he would treat her right and that he would do right by her. She did not (at the time) see that a friend does not treat you the way that Roy was treating her.

Example 3: Petra had prayed for her right man. She had been dating her boyfriend for over 9 years and she kept telling friends that he hadn't yet proposed because marriage just wasn't that important to them both. As Petra and I talked, she began to see that marriage is more than just a promise. It is a covenant between 1 man and 1 woman to enter into holy matrimony and to be there, married and committed to each other, forsaking all others for the rest of their lives. A covenant is a promise in which both man and woman willingly and knowingly enter into an agreement and forsake all others, only being with each other through everything. Petra realized that because her boyfriend was refusing to propose (even after they had had many conversations where she expressed her desire to be married) that his lack of moving things forward was her indication that he was not truly serious about her and that she needed to move forward.

Example 4: Dayanara grew up going to church and to Catholic school. She loved going there because it made her feel happy and connected to God. She felt that she had an excellent relationship with God. Dayanara met Rudolpho outside of church and from the first moment of meeting, he began trying to pull her away from church. He kept inviting her to these "alternate energy meetings" that she was unfamiliar with but being such a kind and trusting person, she went one time to try it out and because she was very interested in Rudolpho. This meeting began talking about very different things and concepts than anything Dayanara had heard about at her Catholic school or in church and she began to feel really confused. Dayanara prayed about this and talked to her church Pastor about these meetings and he let her know that anything taking her away from God and from Jesus was of course not going to be from God. She began to understand that this was the darkness trying to make its way into her life and to deceive her. She promptly ended things with Rudolpho.

Example 5: Fabrizio was very much into Rebecca. He had met her at a church function and was immediately taken by her. Rebecca knew of Fabrizio's interest and wanted to wait just a bit to make sure that this would be a good option for her. Fabrizio and Rebecca began meeting for coffee and talking after Rebecca had spoken to the church Pastor to find out what kind of man Fabrizio was. The Pastor had let Rebecca know that Fabrizio was a very nice man and serious about moving things forward in his life. The Pastor also knew Fabrizio's family and gave his thumbs-up. Rebecca began seriously dating Fabrizio and began, over weeks, to develop the strong sense that this man was God's answer to her prayer request.

Readers, you may be able to see some trends in the case studies I have provided you with. God will not bring you someone who pulls you away from Him and He will not bring you someone who is going to treat you like less-than and yes, stringing you along or ghosting you is treating you like less-than. If you are currently in that kind of relationship, I would advise you and encourage you to rethink that relationship and to know that God loves you, will protect you and will help you. Just ask.

Frequently Asked Questions - answers are in italics

1. Does God hear all prayers?

God hears all prayers, even the ones that you say silently or in your mind.

2. Does God answer all prayers?

God answers all prayers. Every single one of them. The answer can and will come in different forms but they are all answers to your requests and to your prayers.

3. What about people who have chosen not to be married? Do they have a right person too?

If God has called you to be and/or to remain celibate and you have accepted that guidance, then that is your life choice and He will likely not bring you a person unless it is His will to do so at some point for a reason. It is very important to pray about that because He may choose to cause you to be celibate for a time in your life and then things may change.

4. What do you have to say about the stats that say that there are no more good men "out there"?

God knows "the stats" and He doesn't care about them. They are unimportant. There are many good men out there and God knows exactly how to bring you the right one. God also knows exactly how to work on the person so that they are ready for you at the right time.

5. What do I do if I have missed the right one?

Repent (which means say sorry for having missed him or having not following God's promptings) and ask Him if He has any next steps for you. We all have to live with the consequences of our actions (or inactions) but God is also really good at forgiving and helping you move on to what He has next for you.

6. What do I do if I have prayed but I haven't felt, heard or sensed anything?

Keep praying and maybe even go deeper in that prayer. Remember that prayer is a two-way conversation so after you have prayed, sit in stillness and let Him talk to you. Let God know that "I am waiting for You to talk to me, God, and I am looking forward to it." You can also ask Him to be more clear and more obvious in His communications so that He makes sure you don't miss any of it.

7. Will God still answer my prayer if I don't really have a relationship with Him?

Yes, of course but the best thing is to develop that relationship with Him. Contrary to what people may have heard or may think, God is really good and wants what is best for you and as such, whether you already have that relationship with Him or not, He is inviting you into one.

8. I have never had a relationship with God - how will He know what I even want in a man?

You may not have a personal relationship with God but He knows you better than anyone else and loves you more than anyone else can. He already knows everything about you "even the number of hairs on your head" (Luke 12:7) so He knows what you want in a man and what you don't even yet know you really want.

9. Will God bring me the right man if I am divorced or separated?

Of course. Start your personal relationship with Him and you will see how He brings you great things.

10. What if I am in love with two different men and am not sure which one is the right one?

Talk to God about it. Nothing you have felt or can say will be a surprise to Him and He loves you no matter what you have felt or what you have done. When you become close to Him, He will clarify for you in your mind which person is the right person and what to do.

5

If the Answer Is No, Know That There Is a "Yes" Coming!

I really want to make this point very clear: just because you may have gotten a "no" and you know that a man isn't right for you, that's not the end. No need to think "God has forgotten about me and my happiness" or "This man was my last chance."

Quite the contrary.

When you have a "no" answer in front of you regarding someone, that is your golden ticket to realize that there is a "yes" coming. In other words, God doesn't guide you away from one thing without guiding you to something (and in this case someone) else. Your no is your indication that the yes is coming and God will reveal that to you. I know a discouraged woman may be reading this thinking "Easier said than done, Christine. My heart is broken and I thought he was it" but please bear in mind that there will be a "yes" coming soon and that should really excite you. Why should that excite you? Because you know that God is guiding you to the right guy. You just have to listen carefully, pray and follow His prompts.

God's Perfect Design

I believe it is very nice and very comforting to know that God has, in His perfect wisdom, designed things to fit together perfectly. He has designed the world, people, situations and circumstances to fit together perfectly and for everything to work for your best. "And we know that in all things God works for the good of those who love him, who have been called according to his purpose." (Romans 8:28) We may be so used to thinking that this world is in such chaos, that things are so bad "out there" that there is no way I am ever going to meet, be with and fall in love with the right man but you cannot think that way because it does not serve you well nor does it factor in that God can make anything happen for any person at any time. God is not limited to the givens of the current world and He can bring you the greatest happiness out of the worst chaos.

I have watched God bring the greatest good and the great fortune for people who just happened to be there and they weren't at all expecting it. He created the most advantageous situation (for myself included) when I least expected it and at a time when I least thought it would be possible. He brought about a chance meeting with someone on a day that I was busy doing other things and taking care of family matters but then - gasp and alas! - there was a chance meeting just waiting for me! He can bring awesomeness out of any chaos and any situation.

Coming At It From a Place of Faith

What will serve you well is to come from a place of faith and to realize that God has not forgotten about you and He is calling each woman reading this to come to Him, in a loving, personal relationship, and to ask Him who the right man is for you. He is out there and if you are single or will be single and reading this, have faith that God has him in mind for you. If you are attached and are wondering about things, know that He has amazing ways of bringing you comfort, warmth and reassurance in the midst of all that you have going on.

The Guy Isn't A Mind Reader

Now, I want to be clear here when I say this: no man is a mind reader. This means that he will not just automatically know what you mean and what you want. People today are so diverse and so different that even when you think something is a "universal language", know that it isn't. This means that you need to be clear in your communications and not play mind games. When you are committed to looking for and to seeking a great, mature relationship, you cannot be playing mind games. You need to be clear and direct about what you want and you need to make sure that you are communicating with him about what you actually want. This includes your emotional and physical boundaries and limitations.

Many people today erroneously believe that I need to sleep with him in order to "keep him." Please be in the know that your virtue matters and that you should hold steady to the boundaries God has set in His Word. The right man will appreciate that and will honor that. He may playfully see if he can push some boundaries now and then but when it comes down to it, he will respect everything you said you want and need and he will comply with them, even if he doesn't necessarily love it. I have come to realize that men respect you when you set a physical and emotional boundary - it tells them that you respect yourself and that you were honest enough with him to not be playing mind games but to say what you really want and need.

(Romans 8:28) And we know that in all things God works for the good of those who love him, who have been called according to his purpose.

Everything Has Been Factored In

The Scripture passage above is one where we can know, with certainty, that God will be working everything for our favor. Again, going back to my previous point that one might very successfully argue that the world is in terrible shape so how is God supposed to bring me my person in the midst of all of this? He is God and He can bring anything out of anything. That means that He can bring you abundance in a drought, He can bring you joy in the midst of pain and suffering, He can bring you great abundance in the face of great lack. He can make many good things come from not so good things.

Again, none of what is happening in the world is news to God or a surprise to Him. He knew all of what would be happening and

He factored everything in when He created you and him and when He set things up. God controls everything and so when He deems it the right time to bring you your man, it's because He is the God of infinite knowledge and He knows exactly what to do, when to do it and how to do it.

He wants you to rely on Him all the time and for everything.

He wants you to rely on Him all the time and for everything. This means that when He guides you, move forward and go as He has guided.

Using the Opportunity To Grow Your Faith

God wants you to grow. He wants you to increase in faith. He wants you to trust Him and to trust in Him and to know that He will bring you all that you need when you need it (I said when you need it, not necessarily when you want it - big difference). He wants you to rely on Him all the time and for everything. He wants you to rely on His provision for your life…even when it looks like or it is that all the odds are against you. He wants you to grow as a person and for you to develop a better, deeper relationship with Him through personal talks, prayer, reading the Bible, listening to sermons, journaling, reading and practicing devotionals, being good to yourself and to your neighbors, practicing tithing and much more. Just remember to take the appropriate and needed action at the time that it needs to be taken. When you meet someone wonderful, take the action of praying about him and see if he is the right person and then, what you need to do about it.

God bringing you your person will happen differently and may look differently for each person. Some people meet with God's blessings online, some people meet through friends or through family, some people meet in a library or in a bar or in a restaurant, some people fall in love with and marry their best friend from childhood, and the list goes on because the possibilities are so many. God has an amazing and beautiful way of bringing the right guy into your life and that meeting can only happen when God says it's the right time. If it's not the right time and you push things, you will not like what is on the other side of the door. Trust me...I've been there. I pushed and I did not like what was on the other side.

Note: I want to make this point that just because you meet him, it does not necessarily mean that he will be ready or available. Sometimes he will have some things that he needs to work through and he will need some time and/or some help with that. This may mean that he is getting over something, he may be busy with some life changes and he may be battling his own demons. In other words, he may not be available just then and you will have to pray for God to line things up in your favor. This lining up does not usually happen on your timeline but on His.

I remember the case of Barbara. Barbara is a very sweet lady who prayed frequently. When she was getting divorced, she shared with me that she had cried out to God asking Him to bring her her right man. She didn't know who he was and she acknowledged that she did not often like the men she came across so she did not feel like it was very likely for her to meet the right person. A few weeks later, her childhood friend Barney came into her life and shared that he had just lost his wife. Barney had two children but wanted to get remarried so that he could have that happiness back in his life. Barbara knew that her prayer had been answered with Barney but it didn't really look exactly the way she thought it would. She was not looking to become a stepmom and so she had to pray through that before she was able to make such a commitment. The responses she got from her prayers were very clear: Barney was the right guy and stepmom-hood was something she needed to get used to. Within six months, she and Barney had totally reconnected, remembering many of their old times together with happiness and with fondness, and she had met and spent time with his kids and had grown to have a very sweet and mom-like relationship with them. She had grown into the role that God was calling her to and at the same time, God had answered her prayer completely. It just looked differently than what she thought it would look like.

God will answer you but keep in mind that it may not look like you think it will. And that different can be better than you even thought possible.

A woman I know was looking to be with her man with whom she had lost touch with years prior because she had failed to be honest with him about how she was truly feeling. They had lost touch and when they reconnected 20 years later, he shared with her that he had gotten married but was miserable in his marriage and in the way his wife had been treating him for a long time and that he had two children. The woman was not looking to become a step-mom but she had decided that if she wanted to be with this man, that that was something she was going to need to get used to. And she did. She got her wish - it just looked different from how she thought it would look.

Reflection Time

Take a minute right now and in the space provided, use this opportunity to think about what God has put on your heart. Has He guided you to a certain dream? A certain goal? What has He put on your heart? Is there something He has put on your heart that you were unsure about and you'd like some clarification or something that you know God has put on your heart but you have been ignoring or avoiding it? Jot down your notes in the space below. This is very important because you likely felt led to pick up this book for one reason or another and this could be God's way of nudging you to realize that your attention has been away from what He has meant for you.

Activating God's power in your reflection: Use this simple prayer to ask God to bring to your mind anything that He has been trying to impress upon you and that you may not have been paying attention to: *"God, I am coming to You to ask You to illuminate my mind. Has there been something You have been trying to bring to my attention? Has there been something You have been trying to tell me and that I have not followed up on? Bring these things to my mind and show me/ speak to my heart about what You will my next steps to be. In Jesus' name. Amen."*

6

Prepare Yourself

When people want and expect something to come into their lives, it only makes sense to properly prepare for it. Preparing for it means that you will need to put in place all the things that are required for you to successfully accept it and engage with it when you see it present itself. If you want a job, you have to prepare to get it by fixing up your resume, by accepting the job interview, by going for the interview when you get it and by taking the myriad of steps that are required for you to successfully be hired. If you want your right man, you will need to be aware of the qualities you would like (ex. honesty, sense of humor, etc.), you will need to pray for it and you will need to open up space in your life for him. That also means that you will need to take all the steps God is guiding you to take to have that. All the steps.

For example, if you have only ever dated one type of guy and that type of guy is one who is usually a bad boy who puts you down and who treats you as less than you deserve, then preparing yourself would include taking time to foster goodness onto yourself, to be good to you, to go to counseling and work on figuring out why you have attracted and accepted that kind of man and his treatment. It is when we learn to love ourselves that we are in the best position to accept the love of the right man. Know also that when the right guy comes along, you will be very happy if you have taken the time to get ready for him and that will require (for any woman) to do some work in preparing for him - mentally, physically, spiritually and emotionally.

Good men are attracted to women who are good to themselves, who esteem themselves and who can project that by showing that they respect themselves. Good men want to see that you love yourself and that you are taking care of yourself. If you have had a not great history with men or with how you see yourself or even how you have allowed men in the past to treat you, please revisit that and if needed, get some counseling and some support in helping you realize your own value. Your value and your own perceived sense of value is of such tremendous importance and will directly affect how your future relationship with the right man goes. He can treat you like gold but if you don't believe that you are worthy of that, you can destroy that great thing with your own hand.

If you are not sure about this area and you feel that you need some help in your own sense of self, I would recommend some counseling services. Since this is a Christian book, I will suggest getting a Christian counselor. Christian counselors tend to come at things from a Bible-based perspective, and can pray with you as well. With the internet being such a great hub, counseling can easily be done online and so this expands your choice for a counselor considerably.

I want to make it clear here that there is nothing wrong with going for counseling and it does not make you weird, a loser, messed up or any of the other mislabels people can sometimes erroneously use in this situation. Also, pray that God brings you the right counselor because not all counselors will be right for you (and not all counselors are good). Pray and ask God to bring you the right counselor or therapist who will jive well with you, will understand you and will do a fine job in helping you come to a peaceful place of self-love as well as to understand God's love for you.

At times, when some women feel they don't love themselves or they don't love themselves enough, knowing and being reminded of God's love for them is a great starting off point from which their own sense of self will grow.

It's Ok To Cry

In my conversations with many women, they have shared with me that they have felt the need to cry in a session of counseling. That is a good thing. Allowing yourself to have a good, healthy cry can be very conducive to moving forward and can be a great and important step to picking ourselves up.

I also want to add here that it is ok to cry a little bit to mourn a previous relationship or what you thought you had with the person. Let's just be sure that we don't spend all our time or excessive amounts of time mourning a person who ends up not being our Mr. Right - there is no benefit in doing that. It is better to use your time to learn how and why this man is not right for you and then to move forward quickly so that you are not wasting time on the wrong endeavour. We have to preserve our emotions and be good to ourselves and when we spend lots of time mourning the wrong person, we are emotionally exhausting ourselves to no fruitful outcome. Don't spend lots of time mourning him. Move on as God guides and work on yourself.

Positive Words and Positive Affirmations

Speaking positive, motivating and encouraging words over ourselves is so incredibly important. We take to heart the words that we speak and when we speak negatively, we get negatively affected by that. Conversely, **when we speak positively, we get positively affected by that. It is very important that we provide ourselves with the daily positive words and affirmations that are necessary and needed for our development, our self-esteem and our sense of self-worth.**

When we are speaking the positive words, we may not necessarily feel that any change is happening but make no mistake, it is! We are taking the necessary and needed steps of speaking well and positively over our lives and we are letting those good words seep into our conscious and subconscious minds. Good for you!

Here are some examples of words that we can speak over ourselves:

- I am lovely and awesome and worthy
- I am beautiful
- I am athletic

- I am fit
- I am getting emotionally healthier each day
- I am getting physically healthier each day
- I work on my mind fitness each day
- I appreciate myself and I love myself
- I have many great talents and abilities
- I learn and get better each day
- Others appreciate me
- I appreciate me
- Others like me and enjoy my company
- When I know I need to improve in an area, I work on that right away
- The world is blessed to have me in it
- Jesus loves me and thought I was worth dying for
- God created me to be the amazing woman that I am
- I help others each day by being kind and positive to them
- I am good to others even if they are not good to me

Do Unto Others...

Think about it: when we speak good and kind words to others or when we have them speak good and kind words to us, we immediately start to feel happier and so we perk up, we straighten up our backs, we sit up and we feel better about ourselves.

When we take the time to help make others feel good or feel better, we help them out in so many ways. This practice wards off depression, anxiety, feelings of worthlessness, feelings of hopelessness, etc. We need to get into the regular practice of speaking very well over ourselves, even when we don't feel that way. For example, you could be having a bad day and you don't feel like saying your positive words over yourself that day. That is the day where you must say your positive words because it will help you feel better by breaking the cycle of bad and detrimental thoughts. Taking the time to help make others feel better is so good and so important. Both you and the other person benefit from that.

Caught Up In the Day

We can all get so caught up in our day that we forget to take a moment for ourselves. There can and usually are many things vying for our attention so when that happens, remember that you can and should press the pause button and go and spend some time on your own. Go for a walk, drink some water, practice deep breathing, do a workout - many activities that can help break the cycle of bad thoughts that can come over any one of us at any time.

A friend of mine is subject to heart palpitations on a regular basis. She suffers from extreme anxiety and has a really hard time taking that time out to focus on her own wellness. It was only when I absolutely insisted that she make sure that she entered into this practice that she began to take 5 minutes out of her day to do this - and she began to feel better.

Readers, some people like to throw themselves into their work when their love lives are not where they want them to be or when in general, they are not in life where they want to be. There is nothing wrong with distracting yourself but we also have to remember that the body and the mind get tired and will need replenishment. If you don't feed and take care of your body the way it needs, you are going to open the door to many unfortunate perils, not the least of which may be heart palpitations.

Even a little bit of physical activity can make such a great difference in your day. You don't need to become an exercise guru but taking some time each day to work out, especially when you are feeling down or low, is a really important step for your own mental health state of mind. For example, doing cardio (such as walking or running on a treadmill or doing some weights) is not only great for your mental health and well-being but it is also really good for your body and physique.

Grab Your Gratitude Journal

Your gratitude journal is a great place to write down your affirmations, along with what you are grateful for. Remember that your gratitude journal is your feel-good space, the place where you go to remember the wonderful blessings that you have, to remember the difficulties you have been through and have overcome and to help you remember the good things in your life. **No matter where you are in life, you can always think of something or some things that are good in life.**

Don't underestimate the difficulties you have been through, dear reader. You and everyone out there goes through many difficulties and you have to remember how important that experience was. You are a better and stronger person as a result of what you went through and came out on the other side. It is really important to give yourself that little pat on the back and to remember that you have been through that, you survived (and maybe even thrived!) and you came out on the other end! Congrats to you.

Also remember that when you do not take care of yourself, you will be less likely to be the best mate possible for your guy. You cannot forget yourself and do everything for him. You must take the time for yourself and your wellness so that you feel and are the best version of yourself.

Here is a prayer to use to ask God to bring more good into your life: *"God, I am so grateful for all the good You have brought into my life. I thank You deeply. I am asking You to bring me more good things, more happy times, more joy and more excitement into my life. I am asking You to arrange things for me so that each day I live will be filled with joy, with happiness and with things that make me laugh. I ask You to bring me things that will also help me to forget the unfortunate things that have happened in my life. I ask for these things in the name of Jesus. Amen."*

7

Staying Gorgeous

You are beautiful. Stunning. God has created you as a masterpiece.

God created you as the lovely person that you are and I know that God doesn't waste His time or make mistakes.

Might you have some things about yourself that you aren't too crazy about? Sure, you might. I think it's pretty safe to say that many females have that concern but it doesn't mean God made a mistake in creating you. It simply means that you perceive yourself to have some things you would like to improve. God knew He was creating you as an imperfect being but that He considers you to be perfect in His eyes. So when we do things that are contrary to that perfection and that masterpiece, He is saddened and He wishes things would be different.

This chapter on staying gorgeous is all about maintaining your physical and emotional appearance when you are looking to get over him. I write this and make this point because many women feel down about themselves after a breakup or when they find out that a man they were or are interested in isn't the right one. They can tend to neglect themselves a little bit in some areas.

Don't let that be you.

I hope you take this as the compliment it is meant to be : you are a beautiful female and you should show you. You should get your mani-pedi done, your hair looking gorgeous, your skin nice and glowy and all things in place where they need to be and how you would like. You don't need to spend lots of money to do this - simple things can often be the best and you would be taking care of yourself. When we feel happy on the inside, we tend to glow on the outside.

Men Are Visual

This part has to be mentioned at this point in the book: men are very visual and they would like a woman to look attractive, like herself. The right man for you will be attracted to you because you are lovely inside and out - meaning that he loves your look and your personality. So when I say to take care of you and to enhance your already-lovely features, I mean to simply enhance the beauty that is already there, not to cover it up.

If you feel that you have been neglecting this part of you for the last while, let me be the gentle voice that reminds you to get back into that. Take some time for yourself so that you feel good, happy, you feel energized, you feel satisfied and that you are putting your best foot forward.

I remember very clearly when I was trying to get over someone whom I knew very clearly was not the right person for me. I pretty well stopped eating, I spent a lot of time in my room, and I didn't want to see anyone, let alone go out and do such beautifying treatments as getting my nails done. That lasted for a while but I needed to remind myself that I want to look great for myself first and then for my future man. I finally realized that if God says this guy isn't it, then he isn't and that better will come. I had to rely on the character of God to hold onto the promise that love would be coming and that it would manifest. It really helped me get over that particular guy and now, when I look back and I remember my time with him, I realize I shouldn't have spent any time mourning him leaving.

Yes, a man can need some time to grow and to become a better man depending on where he is in life but the right man will not make you feel like garbage and put you down, not to mention take actions that would be hurtful and unacceptable, like hitting and abusing you. If this is you, please take this as your call to action to help yourself out of this situation and to make sure that you safe (or get yourself to a place where you are safe).

Staying Gorgeous On The Inside

When we are feeling hurt and sad, it is a great time to begin doing things that help others. You can take some time to volunteer your time, you can help others, you can do something as simple as complimenting someone you see in the coffee shop. Whatever it is, I want to remind you that when you feel bad about yourself, it's a great time to do something good for someone else. It is as important to stay gorgeous on the inside as it is to stay gorgeous on the outside.

Reflection Time

Take the time in this space to see what God is guiding you to do here. Is He guiding you to give of your time somewhere? Is He guiding you to reconnect with someone? Is He guiding you to spend some time on yourself and to give of your expertise? Take some time and pray and reflect on this.

8

Getting Over Him....Little By Little

I speak from experience when I write this chapter. I have had to get over my fair share of guys. I am one who can fall pretty quickly and then... I have gotten hurt. I know that this is just part of the process of meeting and discovering different people in life and their role in your life. I think it may be fair to say that most women have at some point, had to get over a certain guy for one reason or another. Maybe you found out he wasn't the right guy for you, maybe you found out he was cheating on you, maybe you found out he was keeping things from you or that he had to move away...the list of possible reasons goes on and on. The bottom line is: you know you need to get over him.

So...how do you do that??

You start off small and with little things. You may want to start by deleting his past texts or maybe you start by deleting his pictures off your phone. Taking that first step toward freeing yourself emotionally from him may be a small step but it is also a very important one. The more we begin to remove memories and sights of him, the faster we will start to feel better.

When we begin to slowly extricate ourselves from the wrong person that we need to get over, we then realize that each little step we take toward emotionally detaching ourselves from him will mean that much more to us because it means a step toward the right man. Each time we take a step toward the right man, we should know that that means that we are moving away from wrong and into right.

Patty's story is an example of this. Patty was very excited to have met Dino and she thought (based on their great chemistry) that he would be a great husband. She spent three years with him when she finally realized and admitted that Dino was, in fact, not the right person for her. She knew that based on many inklings and guidance from God after she prayed about their relationship. She felt very confident about this but she was extremely disappointed. She began getting over the relationship by starting to delete his messages, throw out gifts he had given her and pictures they had taken together. She decided that throwing them away would be better and more effective than simply putting them away in storage because she did not want the temptation of knowing that she could go back to the storage space and dig them up and suffer an emotional setback. She shared in a group meeting and counseling session that in hindsight, throwing the items away was effective for her because it eased her emotional burden not to have his items in her home. She had, she felt, fallen deeply in love with him and so she needed to extricate herself completely.

Patty's progress in moving past Dino was wonderful because she was demonstrating strength and she was being realistic with herself about what she needed. Dino, for example, asked to remain close friends but Patty knew that she would not be able to handle that and move on from him. She was being realistic about her needs and I commend her for that. I commend any woman who takes safe and wise steps to emotionally disconnect from the man she knows isn't right for her.

A Personal Story

When I was looking to get over Danny (name changed), I knew I needed to start with getting rid and permanently deleting the pictures of himself that he had sent me. There were tons of his pictures in my phone and I began to see that by keeping his pictures, I was not allowing myself to move on emotionally from this man. I had to set a boundary for how I was going to allow myself to be treated because no man has the power to make you feel bad. We can only allow a man to make us feel bad - that is a choice we make or we can make the choice to not allow that. After the promises I had made to him, I had to make certain promises to myself to value myself and my time from a person who was indicating that he didn't value it or didn't value it enough.

So, I had to peel myself off of the proverbial couch and I had to start the process of getting over someone I felt I really loved. I knew that this would take some time but I also knew that I would be able to get this done. Time does help heal wounds, yes, and praying to God that He takes away your feelings for the person helps also! I knew that I was going to need to take important steps to remove Danny from my life emotionally. So, I began to do all of the following (some were mentioned further up):

- I deleted his many, many, many, many pictures from my phone
- I archived his messages so I wouldn't have to see them
- I deleted his emails
- I didn't look him up on social media
- I put away in the garbage (not storage) all the things I had bought for him because I knew that each item had been bought with love and with care and that that love and care were now being misdirected - they needed to be directed to self-love and to someone else
- I made myself stop thinking about his physical and intellectual features (features of his I admired) so that I could free up space in my mind and in my heart and I did this by getting involved with things meaningful to me
- I deleted my pictures that I took specifically for him and had sent him
- I deleted milestones from my calendar that had anything to do with him
- I wrote good new milestone dates in my phone calendar (ex. Today is the first day I didn't think about Danny at all)
- Any friends who knew about my relationship with him, I asked them to stop asking me about him and to not talk to me about him
- I prayed for God to take away all thoughts of him
- I made a choice to mentally and emotionally let him go by going to a quiet space, holding a balloon in my hand that

represented him and I made the conscious decision to let the balloon go and fly up to the sky, releasing him

The Balloon

What, you may be asking, is the point of the balloon? The point is to be able to have something tangible that I am choosing to let go of for the purposes of an emotional representation of him. By doing this, I am solidifying and confirming the act of releasing him mentally, emotionally and physically so that I can move on from him and in a way that was compelling and meaningful for me. It took me a minute to let go of the balloon (as it may take you) but letting it go felt tremendously freeing and liberating. One might think "it's just a balloon…what's the big deal?" but it was a very powerful step of the moving on process. Doing this allows the balloon to rise away from us and for us to start putting our wellness first.

Each Day Gets Easier

I cannot stress this enough: each day that passes when you are doing this really does make things get easier. I will even go as far as to say that each hour that passes can help you move past him in a great and effective way and then there are the little wins. More on this just below.

> Each step taken means a step in the right direction and in extracating your attachment to him.

I know that at first, this will seem like a hard (and maybe for some, near impossible) task. And that is understandable. You are very close to the situation and that will make it feel and seem harder. Know and take comfort in the fact that when you begin to gain some distance from the situation, and that can mean turning your phone off for a little while, taking a little trip, going to get a cup of coffee and getting away from things....anything that will allow you to move away from the situation for a little while, that task that seemed so impossible will all of a sudden start to feel less impossible and with each passing day, this can get much easier.

With something like this, we have to take a big picture kind of thinking. This means that we have to look at this as not a decision for a month or two or a year or two. We are talking about the rest of your life here. That necessarily means that you need to be very mindful that you are making the right decisions with this and the best (and frankly only) way to do that is to trust a decision and a choice this important to God.

The Little Wins

The little wins are little steps you take each day to move in the right direction. Each step you take toward getting over him is an accomplishment that you are strongly encouraged and invited to celebrate. You could celebrate the deletion of his or his and your pictures, that you didn't need to reread his messages that day, that you didn't go sleuthing through his social media, that you didn't talk about him to your friends and much more. Each step taken means a step in the right direction and in removing your attachment to him. That is a big deal and you should congratulate yourself for each step taken. You may not see it as a big step yet but it is.

Some reading this may feel that celebrating this is silly or pointless. They may think "why would I do that?" You would do that because most humans thrive on rewards and they appreciate them, so with each step you are taking, you are rewarding yourself and that makes a person feel good. This will directly counteract the bad feelings you are likely feeling as you are trying to get over him.

What About Him Were You Not Crazy About?

I say this with respect - in each man we meet, there will likely be things about him that we may not be crazy about. Maybe it was the way he pursed his lips, maybe it was the way he would hog the remote or maybe it was the way he would not clean up after himself. Regardless of what it was about him that you were not crazy about, keeping those things at the forefront of your mind may very well help you move past him and will be helpful in getting you over him. This may seem to some as an unusual way of thinking of things but it does hold true: when we focus on the fact that we won't have that quality of his around anymore, we can make the process of getting over him easier.

Yes, there will be things about the next man that you may not love either but with that man, putting up with these things will be worth it. With this one (the wrong one), you don't need to nor should you put up with those things. Remember, you choose what you will put up with. I have learned that it is only worth it to put up with things from the right man, right as dictated by God.

Reflection Time:

Take some time right now and think about what steps you will take to get over him. Will you delete his past texts? His pictures? Will you let go of a balloon or something like that? What will you keep at the forefront of your mind about what you did not like about him?

9

Closeness To God

One of the most important things I can convey to you, dear reader, is to get close or closer to God. God is the One who loves you the most, knows you the best and will be there for you through anything and everything. Where people fail you, God will not. So, when you are dealing with anything difficult, be it a breakup, a heartache or anything at all, lean into God in prayer and ask Him for help. He will always be there to help you. And then....draw in close to hear what He has to say. God speaks to us all the time but we have to listen. We have to listen carefully and then if there are instructions, we need to exercise our free will and choose to do as we are guided to do.

The Wrong Idea of God

Some people have the wrong idea of God. They assume that He is mean, vengeful, spiteful, unloving and more. People who don't know Him may accuse Him of letting bad things happen in the world, of letting bad things happen to good people, of letting death and destruction come into the world and so much more. Some may say that God is difficult, not inclusive and more.

God created us to have free will and this means that we have at our disposal the ability to choose for ourselves, to create goodness or to create destruction in the world and more. We can either sow and reap good or we can sow and reap negative things. God wants everyone to feel included and loved.....He is love! But we also have to be mindful that like a good parent, there are rules that we have to follow so that we don't fall into bad habits, so that we respect human life and so that we can make sure that we can be sure that we are being inclusive. This means that we should not be shooting up schools, that we should respect the right to life and that people can be anything they want to be but they are encouraged to choose being good and doing good unto others.

When we choose things that are not positive, we will reap the effects of those things. So let's not blame God for the not so great choices humans make.

Check out all of the following cases and see what happened when the person did follow through on the instructions provided and when they didn't:

- Marianna prayed deeply for help in discovering whether her husband was the right person for her. She had not had a relationship with God growing up and so she didn't know whether the man she had married years ago was actually the right man for her. She had prayed about this and received a strong sensation that he was the right person. Marianna was not satisfied with this, however, and she began to have a strong attraction to a male co-worker. When the co-worker invited her to get coffee during one of their breaks, she happily accepted and the flirting and innuendos began. As Marianna moved closer and closer to her coworker, she began to become more and more emotionally unavailable to her husband. Her husband sensed this distance and talked to her about it but Marianna just blew it off as he was being too sensitive. After weeks of coffee break outings and flirting, Marianna's coworker made a move on her and kissed her. She kissed him back, knowing this was not right and knowing that she was breaking her marriage vows and in the meantime, also hurting her husband if he ever found out. This continued for weeks and the kissing turned into more and Marianna moved further and further away emotionally, mentally and physically from her husband. She was making a clear choice to move away from the right man. She was ignoring the negative feelings that she was experiencing, urging her to stop doing these things and to focus on her marriage and on the man she knew was right for her. In the end, the new love interest Marianna was engaging in dropped her and moved onto someone new, leaving her marriage completely broken and her husband heartbroken. She had chosen (very unfortunately) to ignore the warning signs.

- When Josephine was considering marrying Eduart, she went to her Parish Priest to ask for his blessing. Her Parish Priest did the right thing by letting her know that he would pray over their relationship to determine if Eduart was the right person for her. Josephine thanked the Priest and let him know that she would be awaiting his response. A week passed and the Priest called Josephine. He did indeed believe that Eduart was the right man for her but that he sensed strongly that they had some differences that would need to be worked through. The Priest suggested free (through the Church) marriage classes and while Josephine was really happy about the answer about Eduart, she was unwilling to attend the marriage classes. "We don't need that stuff....Eddie and I are really good," she told the Priest. The Priest again suggested that they really should attend the classes, that they were free and that perhaps she should at least discuss the classes with Eduart. "No, that's ok" insisted Josephine. A few months into their marriage, Josephine began to understand why the Priest had suggested the marriage classes. There were some things in her history that were making it very challenging for her to maintain her relationship with Eduart and that without dealing with those things in her past (and making Eduart a party in her recovery), this was not going to end well. Josephine chose to "work through" the issues on her own with a counselor who did not know the information the Priest had gotten and so Josephine's counseling sessions were not dealing with the issues that were pressing. This is an example of how a person chose to go their own way and not listen to the wisdom and advice of God that they themselves had asked for.

- When Bernice met Horatio online, she thought it was love at first click. She was nuts about him and they were getting along wonderfully well. Bernice was ignoring the signs that Horatio was displaying that indicated a bit too much jealousy and possessiveness. When they met up for a date, Bernice got a little bit afraid at how Horatio would stare down any guy who even walked near Bernice but despite her uneasiness, she continued to date Horatio, assuming that he was just showing her how much he cared about her. When friends began expressing a bit of concern about Horatio's temper, Bernice simply said "he enjoys me all to himself". Bernice was missing the signs from God that this man may not be right for her and that he may actually be a bit dangerous. It was only after the first time he slapped her that she began to see that his "caring" was actually low self esteem on his part and that his possessiveness over her was just his way of trying to make sure that she didn't leave him. Bernice had an important choice to make about whether she would let Horatio keep treating her like that or whether she would go on to be with the right man who would treat her the right way.

See It For What It Is

You see, dear reader, when you begin to allow yourself to have a relationship with God, you begin to know Him and you begin to trust Him. You may likely begin to see yourself as the wonderful masterpiece He created you to be and you may begin to attract people into your life who reflect that way of seeing yourself.

We have to love ourselves enough to allow ourselves to have that active relationship with God because He is:

- Our Provider
- Our Father
- Our Helper
- Our Savior

- Our Counselor
- Our Friend
- Our Source
- Our Jehovah Jireh
- Our Confidant
- Our Way-Maker

When you have that active and personal relationship with Him, it will be much easier to identify the right people who should be in your life versus the wrong people who have no place in your life. The truth about people and situations becomes clear (sometimes to our shock) and we begin to see that God helps us navigate situations and people in truth. He will tell you if this guy is right for you or if he is not, and if he isn't, He will help you get over him and move on to the right man.

Trust in HIM!

Reflection Time: Take some time right now and jot down in the space provided some of your thoughts on how close you are to God. Are you as close to Him as you would like to be? Do you go to Him when you are facing challenges and struggles or do you try to handle them all on your own? Do you go to Him when you are not sure about something and don't know how to proceed? Or do you try to make God fit your mold of how you think He should be? Will you try to listen to some sermons and discover more about the loving personality and nature of God? Which ones will you listen to?

10

Success!

I want to congratulate you, ladies, on taking an important step toward living your best life!

It is so important that we live our lives based on how God guides us, what He tells us, the ways He speaks to us about and the perils and pitfalls that we each find along our journey. We only see part of what is going on around us. God sees all of it and so when we take all matters into our own hands, we are missing a significant part of the equation. Maybe it's the part of the equation that we can't see yet but it is still important to know about it.

I also want to congratulate you for taking the steps necessary to hold your heart and your love for the right man. This is so important (especially in our world today) and when we trust in God and we do as He says, even in the midst of challenges, we will come out victorious. If your spouse or boyfriend or the man you are seeing is not on the same God-page, here is a prayer you can pray that will help with that: *"God, You know that _____ is the man I am seeing/dating/considering marrying. You know his heart and that he is not a praying man or not a man who relies on faith. I am asking You, in Your way, to speak to his heart and to reveal Yourself to him so that he becomes a man of faith, one who seeks to pray with me, to trust in You with me and to include You in our relationship journey. I am asking You to change his heart and to help him be the man You know he needs to be, by giving him what he needs to believe in You. I desire to take on this next venture with You and so I hope that my right man will also want to do this with me. I thank You in advance and pray for these things in the name of Jesus. Amen."*

Congratulations on your success! I wish you much continued success.

Pay It Forward

If this book and its teachings help(ed) you in any way and you know of a friend, colleague or family member who would benefit from its timely teachings, please do pass it on to them. I pray that this book helps as many women as possible to find her right guy and to move on safely and well from the wrong, while at the same time finding her close relationship with God.

If you can think of 5 people who would benefit from the teachings in this book, write their names down in the space provided. If you feel led to do so, write down how you can let them know about this book and how it can help them on their journey.

Some ways you can share this book with them:
- take a picture with your phone of a page or a section and send it to them
- take a picture of the cover and send it to them with a caption "I lovingly think this book can help you"
- just telling them about the book
- buy a copy of the book for them and deliver it to them in an appropriate way
- tell them about my website (www.drchristinetopjian.com) so that they can find more helpful resources and tips
- send them a blurb about how the book's teachings helped you

- read a section of the book to them and send the audio file to them

- create a visual drawing or schema of one of the book's teachings and invite them to work with that

Remember, when we do something good unto others, it is just a matter of time until God makes sure that you receive your reward for that good thing. It doesn't mean the reward will come from the same person to whom you did the good deed but it will come back to you because that is one of God's laws.

The Names of 5 People:

About Dr. Topjian

Dr. Christine Topjian is a multi-award winning author of many books in the areas of faith, visualization, manifesting, finance and money, love and more. Her books are meant to be a how-to guide for people all over the world on how to live their best lives with God. Her books all have God at their core.

She has completed her first Doctorate in Prophetic Ministry (Christian Leadership University) and she is (as of this book's writing) working on her second in Christian Leadership (Christian Leadership University).

Christine is an avid follower of God, prays each day and is engaged in the process of meditating each day. "Meditation and prayer for me are absolutely essential, as they are practices that allow me to feel good, to get things off my chest by talking to God and both go a long way to helping me achieve (with God's help and grace) all that I believe I am guided to achieve in this life. There is no limit to God's goodness so why would there be a limit to the good He wants for each of our lives?"

Christine lives in Thornhill, ON with her family and runs the website, www.drchristinetopjian.com.

About Dr. Topjian

Other Books From the Author

Here are some more books from the author:

The Chrissie Series: Chrissie Meditates & Visualizes

The Chrissie Series: Chrissie Speaks Nicely

The Chrissie Series: Chrissie Prays

Love & Kindness

The Money Manual

Manifest It

Manifest It...Now!

Are You Ready for God's Best?

Jesus Loves You

Give It To God

Other Books From the Author

The Art of Getting It Done: Secrets of Overachievers and How Anyone Can Be One

How To Be Led by the Holy Spirit

God & Prosperity

Etes-vous prets pour le meilleur de Dieu? (French edition)

The Ontario Residential Real Estate How-To Book

The Smart Series: Taking Smart Risks

The Power of the Give (an illustrated book)

It's in Transit

How To Get Over The Wrong Guy: A Book for Women

www.ingramcontent.com/pod-product-compliance
Lightning Source LLC
Chambersburg PA
CBHW050247010526
44107CB00003B/214